Image &
Imagination

Image & Imagination is published by Switch Press
A Capstone Imprint
1710 Roe Crest Drive, North Mankato, Minnesota 56003
www.mycapstone.com

Library of Congress Cataloging-in-Publication Data
Names: Healy, Nick, author. | McCurry, Kristen, author.
Title: Image & imagination / by Nick Healy and Kristen McCurry.
Other titles: Image and imagination
Description: North Mankato, Minnesota : Switch Press, a Capstone imprint,
   [2016] | Audience: Ages 14-18. | Audience: Grades 9 to 12.
Identifiers: LCCN 2015039876 | ISBN 9781630790448 (pbk.)
Subjects: LCSH: Creative writing–Juvenile literature. |
   Photographs–Juvenile literature.
Classification: LCC LB1576 .H3265 2016 | DDC 808–dc23
LC record available at http://lccn.loc.gov/2015039876

Image Credits:

iStockphoto: double_p, mabus13; Shutterstock: Africa Studio, Alex Emanuel
Koch, Alexander Piragis, Ammentorp Photography, Amos Struck, Andrey Vishin,
Aneta_Gu, Anna Paff, Anton_Ivanov, Arsgera, Balazs Images, Blulz60, blurAZ,
Brian A Jackson, cagi, Catalin Petolea, CHOATphotographer, Christian Mueller,
coloursinmylife, Cranach, Creative Travel Projects, Crystal Home, David Fossier,
DavidTB, Denis Rozhnovsky, designelements, Dirima, Dmitrijs Dmitrijevs, Dora
Zett, Dudarev Mikhail, Ellerslie, Elovich, Everett Collection, Everett Historical,
Frontpage, Galyamin Sergej, Gil,amshin, Glenda, gurinaleksandr, hecke61, hikrcn,
hurricanehank, ian, iBrave, IgorGolovniov, imagemaker, In Tune, Ivan Chudakov,
Jakub Krechowicz, Jixin YU, Joe Mercier, Jose AS Reyes, Jueg Schreiter, Julia
Karo, kaca kaca, karnizz, Karuka, Kevin L Chesson, Kichigin, kim7, konmesa,
krsmanovic, kryzhov, Kunal Mehta, lassedesignen, leungchopan, Lolostock,
luminaimages, Maria Dryfhout, Masson, Maxisport, meawnamacat, Mike Flippo,
Mila Supinskaya, MJTH, Monkey Business Images, Mr.Zara, mycteria, Nonwarit,
Oclacia, OliverSved, Ollyy, P3k, Passion Images, Patrick Foto, Patrizia Tilly,
Phil MacD Photography, Piotr Gatlik, pjhpix, Polina Ledneva, prugkov, R.M.
Nunes, Riccardo Mayer, roibu, ronstik, Roxana Bashyrova, Ryan Rodrick Beiler,
S.Borisov, S.Pytel, Serghei Starus, solominviktor, Storimages, Suzanne Tucker,
szefel, T.Dallas, Tana Lee Alves, tomertu, triocean, tsaplia, TTstudio, Valentina
Photos, VladisChem, Volodymyr Ivash, yexelA, Zurijeta

Design Elements: Capstone and Shutterstock

Printed in China.
092015   009231S16

Image & Imagination

Ideas and Inspiration for Teen Writers

by Nick Healy and Kristen McCurry

SWITCH PRESS

an imprint of capstone

Introduction

If you want to write, you probably know it can be a pleasure, a thrill, and a laugh. You might also know it can be a struggle, and that often the struggle begins before you get your first sentence on the page. When your life buzzes with constant sharing, posting, tweeting, etc. (so many words!), how do you know what's worthy of something more? How do you know when you've got the perfect idea? How do you get started?

The truth is, the universe offers us very few perfect ideas, but our world produces lots of good ideas—interesting, surprising, and fresh ones. As most experienced writers will tell you, the way to uncover gems amid rubble is by writing your way to them. You may grind out a thousand words before you discover the trail you want to follow.

You may need to lay down only a sentence or two before reaching that point. Either way, the work that gets you going is worth it.

Most writers quickly discover that the process includes three phases—getting your words onto paper, shaping them into something that really glows, and sharing them with other people. This book is all about that first step—and that part is the most fun.

Yes, the process of creating something new, something entirely your own, can be fun. Lots of it. So let down your guard. Use the wild mix of prompts and photos in this book to get yourself started. Don't hesitate. Don't doubt. Don't worry. Just choose a path and follow it.

How do I use this book?

Simple. However you want. You will find space to write near each prompt, and you're free to jot ideas anywhere you want.

What should I write?

That's what the nearly 150 prompts–ideas, tips, story starters, examples, and more–are for. Some of them ask you to dig deep inside and pull those hidden thoughts out into the open (or at least onto the friendly pages of this book). Others ask you to create something entirely new–write a scene, describe a character, write a poem, make up some bold and bizarre stuff. Still others offer inspiring quotes that might blow your mind if you think about them too hard.

This isn't a workbook, and you don't have to do what the prompts ask. You don't have to follow any rules. But images and ideas you'll encounter can be a starting point. The idea is to get you thinking, get your fingers twitching, get your pen moving.

Write big. Write small. Write fancy (cursive, anyone?). Or scribble. If you run out of room or have SO MUCH to say about a particular idea, flip to the end of the book and write some more. There's extra space back there.

Share what you write with others or hide it under your mattress for all eternity. Trade it back and forth with your best friend or leave it lying around the house and see what happens. This book is yours to do with what you want. The only requirement is that you WRITE.

Oh, and don't forget
to have fun. Go!

Describe your top three magical moments.

Explain the difference
between how the world
sees you and how you are.

Lissa saw it before her friends did,

but she didn't know what she was seeing.

Tell the story of what happened next.

I laughed
so hard
when ...

When is it worth the risk?

You are the chosen one.
What is your destiny?

Liam finally kissed her,

and it was ...

Write a poem about the last day of school.

what's your favorite word? why?

When she heard the words "Don't try this at home," Katie **always** did.

Write a profile of this character.

List the five things you feel most passionate about.

It was love. True love! But she had a secret.

Write her note of confession.

To write action, put things in slow motion. Use simple sentences. Describe the character's moves. Show them step by step. Explain what he's thinking. Be sure to mention what he hears. Don't forget the burning in his lungs and in the muscles of his legs.

I feel fragile when ...

Write a poem or story about a
time you got caught in the rain.

You're writing a story, not a police description. Give readers one or two specific and memorable details about a face, and they will imagine a whole face—even a whole person.

In one sentence, provide one or two details that show us a handsome face.

Now show us a frightening one.

"The world," he said, "is not a wish-granting factory."

–John Green, The Fault in Our Stars

In your opinion, what else is the world not?

What *is* the world, then?

He smiled for the camera because he knew he should. Write a paragraph about what he's really thinking.

Begin this way:
Conditions weren't ideal,
but I made it work.

He thought he could explain the meaning of life in a single sentence. He said, "We're like dust in the spotlight."

She said, "You're not as clever as you think."

Write the rest of the conversation.

Yes or no? Go.

Write this story:

She couldn't see anyone, but she knew she was being followed.

continue this story:

When her driver's ed instructor fell asleep, Emma had a few options.

what do you think about when you hear your favorite song?

He is the first person to set foot in this place in centuries. What brought him here?

Give yourself 100 words
to answer this question.

What is your story?

Are they traveling entertainers? Wealthy merchants? Dastardly criminal masterminds? Members of a secret society? You decide. Imagine and explain the history of this family.

Sonya went into her brother's bedroom,
looking for a book. What she found was a
secret she didn't know if she should keep.

What did she find? What did she do next?

I will never live down the time I ...

Describe something you can do that most people can't.

Continue this story:
She said she would be the one with the red umbrella, but I found only the umbrella.

What is your

Write a story about a world in which it is good for you.

She had been expecting this news for some time.
What message did she receive?

Solve one of the world's problems in 25 words or less.

Most of them were simple pieces of jewelry. She had to find the one that was a vessel of great magic.

Start her story here:

There were thousands of cards, and each one listed the title and location

Write a paragraph:

of a book. Only one of those books could tell her what she needed to know.

When do you feel most alive? When do you feel most alone?

Something sinister
invaded Lyla's room.
Write a paragraph
in its voice.

Desert island list:

If you could take only 10 possessions with you,
what would they be?

1.

2.

3.

4.

5.

6.

7.

8.

9.

10.

Write a poem about the
person who lives here.

Write a six-word story about this:

Describe the last dream you remember.

names matter.

What's her name?

What's her name if she's a liar?

What if she's a saint?

If she's a true friend?

Or a snake?

If she's innocent?

If she's not?

If she works at Burger King?

If she's never worked a day in her life?

Something I hoped they'd NEVER find out ...

Imagine your grandparents' first date. What did they talk about?

Write the dialogue.

What makes love last?

Shelby knew she was in trouble,
but she didn't know how much.
What was her crime?

The human body is

bizarre.

If you could redesign the human body, what would you leave out?

A portal has appeared in Jackson's closet.
Where does it lead? What does he do?

The cat was watching Max again. What did it see?

Everybody is a **genius**. But if you judge a fish by its ability to climb a tree, it will live its whole life believing that it is **stupid**.

—Anonymous

Write a paragraph about
a person in your life
whose gifts are ignored
or misunderstood.

What happens when humans are unnecessary?

Cody wore one face with his friends,
but it felt like a mask.

Tell his story:

Describe euphoria.

How are you strange?

How are you powerful?

THE FIRST
TIME
I TRIED
COFFEE ...

The Greater New York
Philanthropic Society
The One Cent Coffee Stands

You wake up here.
What do you hear?

If you could save only one photo
of yourself, what would it show?

People think I'm ...

Andre thinks something is wrong with his new cell phone, but soon he realizes it allows him to hear his neighbors' conversations. He discovers these people are not what they seem. Write dialogue for a conversation Andre overhears. Build a story from his neighbors' secrets.

Create a scene based on a memorable moment in your childhood—a single, small event. Don't start by telling the reader what happened. Show people talking and taking action, and let the reader witness events as they unfold.

What advice would you like to give to your 7-year-old self?

Give this story a happy ending.

The sun blinked at us and we blinked back.
Outside smelled like perfect leaves, the air clean
and breathy, so we crossed to Boris Vian Park
and looked at what we had. It was a magical thing ...
—Daniel Handler, Why We Broke Up

Notice how the author blends description with action, and how details about the setting support the happy mood. Write a scene that begins like this but under darker circumstances ...

write the playlist for your perfect day.

(Then write the playlist for your funeral.)

Describe this scene without using the word "rainbow" or naming any colors.

Weird things I've done to get a laugh include but are not limited to ...

Happiness is like a butterfly. The more you chase it, the more it eludes you. But if you turn your attention to other things, it comes and sits softly on your shoulder.

—Anonymous

Write your own simile to explain happiness in your life.

Write a short poem about the coldest day of winter.

You've got to do your own growing, no matter how tall your grandfather was.
—Irish proverb

Write a story or poem about a 16-year-old guy learning this lesson the hard way.

What is the worst thing
you've ever done?

[Write in tiny letters.]

The beach was hours away by bicycle, forbidden, completely out of all bounds. Going there risked expulsion, destroyed the studying I was going to do for an important test the next morning, blasted the reasonable amount of order I wanted to maintain in my life, and it also involved the kind of long, labored bicycle ride I hated. "All right", I said.

—John Knowles, A Separate Peace

Write a scene in which your character thinks one thing but says the opposite.

Worst day ever. Explain yours.

Tell me, what is it you plan to do
with your one wild and precious life?
—poet Mary Oliver

If you could choose one superpower—invisibility or flight—which would you choose and what would you do with it?

Begin this way: She wondered if she was the only one who could see the hidden message.

Imagine an ancient city on its last day.
Tell the story of what happens.

And those who were seen dancing were thought to be insane by those who couldn't hear the music.

—popular adage often attributed to philosopher Friedrich Nietzsche

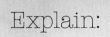

Explain:

This time, when she woke up, she was in the middle of nowhere, and she was in a boy's body.

Who is she and why is this happening?

What's your problem?

Write about something that's a beautiful, crazy mess.

Love is a
Beautiful crazy mess.
— M

A reader lives a thousand lives before he dies ... The man who never reads lives only one. —author George R. R. Martin

List 10 books you've lived and loved:

Tell the villain's
side of the
story.

Spin the globe. If you could go anywhere, where would it be?

List five places you dream of visiting:

Begin your story with this familiar line:
It was a dark and stormy night.
(Make the next sentence surprising.)

Life without screens begins tomorrow.

Explain how you're a prisoner to screens:

Describe your life without them:

Before I met Reeve and wanted to be with him all the time, my closest friends in Crampton were two other low-key, nice girls with long, straight hair—girls like me.
—Meg Wolitzer, Belzhar

List everything you learn from this sentence. Then write a sentence that says a lot about a character you've imagined.

What's your favorite
furry friend memory?

What is the thing you want to announce to the world?

Start writing with a question.
Write toward an answer. If you
reach the answer too easily,
rephrase your question.
—author Pete Hautman

Write five questions
based on this scene.

1.

2.

3.

4.

5.

In three words I can sum up everything
I've learned about life: It goes on.
—poet Robert Frost

What would your three words be? Why?

The house was lovely and new when Trudy's family moved in long ago.
She had just turned 14, and her life was getting better and better.
Write her diary entry from that day.

Don't forget about color. You're painting a picture with words, and your painting should have color. Give yourself 50 words to describe this character and setting.

The five people on
Earth I wouldn't
want to live without:

The world is ending. What do you do?

Write a message to a long-lost friend:

If you have kids someday, what will you warn them about?

Explain the plot of your favorite book or movie in three sentences.

Now imagine a story that ends in this deserted place.
Summarize the plot in three sentences.

Write a scene in which the landscape
takes your character's breath away.

*It was enough just to sit
there without words.*

–author Louise Erdrich

Dogs are better than human beings
because they know but do not tell.

—poet Emily Dickinson

What does your pet know about you that
no one else does?

It was a body capable
of enormous leverage ...

– F. Scott Fitzgerald, The Great Gatsby

Imagine a character and write a one-sentence description that captures your character's body and its capabilities.

This is what happened the time I told
the voice in my head to shut up ...

Write a thank-you letter to the person who always has your back.

What is
something
you'd like to
do if only you
had the guts?

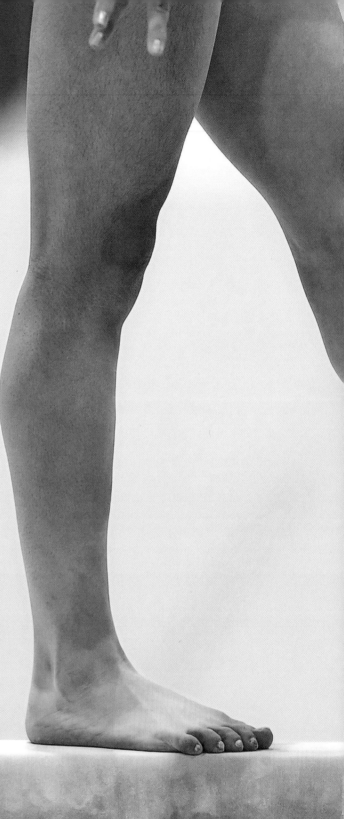

You miss 100%.
of the shots you
don't take.

-hockey star Wayne Gretzky

write about a time you should've but didn't.

He appeared out of nowhere one day.
He couldn't say where he came from.
Tell his story.

Begin this way: He would probably regret it, but that's what made it fun.

She carried the photograph with her always because it reminded her of the time before the war.

Give your character an important possession and explain why it matters to him or her.

A larger crowd made its way around them as Rudy swung at Franz Deutscher's stomach, missing him completely. Simultaneously, he felt the burning sensation of a fist on his left eye socket. It arrived with sparks, and he was on the ground before he even realized.

—Markus Zusak, The Book Thief

Describe the feeling of impact.

Storseisundbrua

I THOUGHT
I WOULD
NEVER
MAKE IT.

Write about a moment when this was true for you.

Don't tell me the moon is shining; show me the glint of light on broken glass.

—author Anton Chekhov

Describe your neighborhood under the light of a full moon.

Write a story that begins with this sentence: He couldn't speak the language, but he could go anywhere he pleased.

bring these kids to life.

What would they say to each other?

Where would they go?

What's holding you back?

Keep going!

What's holding you back?
- In the case of love, Fear & Rejection hold me back
  from admitting personally to my crush that i like him.
  Love is beautiful, yet complicated.

To: Octavio Montes De Oca Perez (I like you)!!

There is no greater agony than bearing an untold story inside you. —Maya Angelou

I always do my draft in longhand because even the ink is part of the flow. —Martin Amis

To me, the greatest pleasure of writing is not what it's about,
but the inner music that words make. —Truman Capote

Don't loaf and invite inspiration; light out after it with a club. —Jack London

We write to taste life twice, in the moment and in retrospection. —Anaïs Nin

If there's a book that you want to read, but it hasn't been
written yet, then you must write it. —Toni Morrison

About the authors:

Nick Healy is a writer and editor in Mankato, Minnesota, where he also teaches creative writing at Minnesota State University. He has written and edited many books for young readers, and he's the author of *It Takes You Over*, a short-story collection that received a 2013 Friends of American Writers Literary Award.

Kristen McCurry is an editor and author with a lifelong love of children's and young-adult books and topics. She has a husband, two kids, and a beagle, and she keeps a towering stack of books on her nightstand that often topples in the middle of night, frightening her family. She lives in Minnesota near one of the 10,000 lakes.

Kristen and Nick co-edited *Love & Profanity*, a collection of true stories about teenage life, released in March 2015.